city treaty

city treaty

by
marvin francis

TURNSTONE PRESS

city treaty
Copyright © Marvin Francis 2002

Turnstone Press Ltd.
607-100 Arthur Street
Artspace Building
Winnipeg, MB
R3B 1H3 Canada
www.TurnstonePress.com

Turnstone Press gratefully acknowledges the assistance of The Canada Council for the Arts, the Manitoba Arts Council, the Government of Canada through the Book Publishing Industry Development Program and the Government of Manitoba through the Department of Culture, Heritage and Tourism, Arts Branch for our publishing activities.

Canada

Cover detail: "Museum, drunk tanks, booscans, and bank" by Roger Crait
Design: Sharon Caseburg
Printed and bound in Canada by Friesens for Turnstone Press.

Second printing: August 2003

National Library of Canada Cataloguing in Publication Data

Marvin Francis, 1955-
City treaty

A poem.
ISBN 0-88801-268-3
I. Title
PS8561.R2586C57 2002   C811'.6   C2002-910083-6
PR9199.4.F72C57 2002

to the people of Heart Lake

special thanks to david arnason
and dennis cooley and
other professors and students from the U of Manitoba and the
U of Winnipeg
and the Aboriginal Writers Collective
and the Urban Shaman Gallery

and the old furby street musicians

and dorothy and john and robert and georgina and big marvin
who understand my craziness

and all the people of Heart Lake

to samahra and samantha who had to live this manuscript

to all those from Turnstone

and most

especially

to cindy

who lets me
be me

city treaty

e-
nters pulls
bag takes out toy cow-
boys   plastic indian
head dress adjustment

good evening everyone   my name is Joe.
jOE tb, you know, tb, treaty buster, i am
a bush poet, i got one lung left. i can
prove it, i know twenty words that rhyme
with moose, i can prove it

loose   goose   spruce

sluice bruce noose

deuce deuce
matoose (cheap sweet wine)
chartreuse (expensive green)
excuse shingoose zeus
papoose   abuse!
snoose (is this a canuck word)
obtuse caboose reduce seduce va-
moose
but not truce never never truce
cuz i am a treaty buster

I was being followed

so I took my usual back alley route

trash can trails

make 'em get their feet dirty

but it was no use

you cannot shake a clown

that mask sees all

we began the treaty project

we needed money we wrote

on the back maize   flake boxes   expensive

the clown

knows ever since sky   ripples

mingles clown   city native

write new treaty   cost heap big money

the clown surveys post/city/modern/after treaty/after

lawyer = life

and finds

the way

to finance

this project

finds the reality:

mcPemmican [TM1]

first you get the grease from canola buffalo

then you find mystery meat

you must package this in

bright colours   just like beads

let the poor intake their money take their health

sound familiar

chase fast food off the cliff

speed beef

deer on a bun

bury in the ground

special this day

mcPemmican[TM]

cash those icons in

how about a

mcTreaty[TM]

would you like some lies with that?

[1] treaty manuscript

they line up for blocks   dying to clog mind arteries everyone has

at least one fortieth indian↓ two parts water   the rest unknown

they line to see the real   ↑to buy the grey owl burger

to touch the other   money did fall

                    from the sky

        we had one table reserved by the window we write

                        the city treaty

country words   me and this clown

            pencils sharp   look busy   act important

                    look out the window

        so you have to explain who is this clown

                        but I won't

                        I can knot

                    will not will not

                    just like hem

                        ing way

                        instead

                        we found

                        some

Treaty Lines

all from actual treaties   all emerge into the native

aboriginal   first nation   last chance   indian status   cuz

you went trapping that day   universe

1677-virginia-violent intrusions of divers English forceing the Indians
to kill the Cattle and hogs

         me: they like to hunt those short squealing buffalo

               clown: it's a living

the english dive into land   they need
Steal **C**ountry **U**sually **B**ecause **A**ll is ours

the bubbles explode upward   come up for
heirs

did james hogg die crossing the atlantic

1868   fort laramie → they will not attack any persons at home or
travelling, nor molest any wagon trains, mules or cattle

wagon molestation connects you to one of the largest
tribes
the prison tribe

Court Transcripts

(trans. g. reega)

judge: why did you do it?

clown: they put the wagons in a square circle and I just lost it,

man

me: this little red wagon followed me home when I was a kid

caught me in the park and I was never the same after that

judge: do not pass go

do not   collect   five dollars   per year   free parking

no wagons

one thousand seven hundred and eighty-four → *fort stanwix* → *six*
hostages will be delivered to the commissioners by the said nations

who gets to go

hear they got food

pick him   pick her   pick axe   pick a name

the w. redskins (some colour change may apply, colours may run)

the c. indians (the intelligent mascot)

the a. braves (tom a. hwk. chp)

the kc chiefs (they be in charge, should be in vegas)

the und fighting sue (not peggy)

the c. black hawks (t-shirts and all that)

just pick one

six word prisoners assemble   sit in circle   one remains

she sits in smaller circle they drink tea in a tree   tree T

when asked how they got treated in the big city they said those

people scrape the sky

with cement and

out

  falls

      a

           clown

           all arms and legs

when this clown sees the skies scrape   thinks aloud

big family,   huh

and that is when we met   that is the treaty   so far

intensive research leads   tense words

              paper burns trail

          paper chase   rabbit fonts

names every   where   too many

             until

               the clown jumps up from the net

                  I found that common denominator

            sea links to bush to red sea   one collective tribe

all the chiefs those head (wo) men   captain

those red names   white language

they all share

the same last

name:

HIS MARK.

treaty names

all duly hit the mark

all treaty team

running wolf   *wolf collar*   *sam wolf*

history howls this new story line

walking through the bush narrative

read the bodies behind the totems

the marks so important

red crow   *eagle rib*   *jon chicken*   *crow collar*

hitch the wagons

cock bird terror

northern love bird

cause

feather fantasy   crow turns colour

the clown stops for mcBannock

paces while I struggle

for names

wants to know

what is a nick name

so I explain

a nick name has

a little piece of you

and sometimes you must run

away from home to

lose that name

this causes mask to fall

off but the next mask

now looks at me

Uses Both Arms   *Sometimes Glad*   *Cake Cake*

the translator hold his head and cries

nobody believes me

thick foot   the original

crow $ $ foot
white eagle
white pup

say say sew say it aint so, chief
the captive
bad head (sure is different this millennium)
sun rise   two guns
dodging a horse   hit first
afraid of grass hopper

help us amigos

they trap us in this

leg and neck and soul hold

trap

we live in circles

we die   in this square   piece of paper

trick or treaty

halloween apples red outside

white inside but

maybe a disguise

word razor blades

how many skid row tricks are native

open the door so you can see

my indian costume

buck knife buckaroo buck naked buck skin pass me my buck

back

fringes torn from skin   theatre fringe   half dance   part story

oral fringe

the best halloween prop

a native dogstory

"we rode our bikes, man, and twenty dogs came running,

tore my cowboy boot right off, man"

"that's nothing, we were riding this d-freaking-nine-cat

no cab or fuckall, and those dogs, raised on diesel, kill the

foreman, rip that white hat to shreds"

my dogstory?   insert mad dog right here

the mad dog

across the dirty creek lives boris

meanest bark disturbs the water

we learn he breaks his rope

his smell breath smell

mean teeth stretch anger

so invite new kids

those that came to indulge

sudden chance to learn

boris can

jump onto the pulp

truck too

watch through innocent

smiles

the red anger

of

d

o

g

we knew why

so hungry   so cruel

rage of master

yellow teeth

boris tears open paper boy

we give out a ragged cheer

and hide

in the bush when the

cops come

those sad shots by our

door our mind became smug

we always knew they would

shoot the wrong dog

master drinks red

dawg beer

ggrowls into his children

sslobber and

dddroooo

oool

lead meets dog

and sure

enough

limp and growl   limp and growl

boris came back that

night

howl

at the meanest dog

that lives across

the dirty creek

INT. – mcPemmican – late nite

clown: inner city trick walk into convenience

store wear a mask   legally

DISSOLVE TO:

INT. – mcPemmican – early morning

me: this halloween I am

going as mickey

indian

CUT TO:

booze treaty

time for some

new   beer labels

catch the redeye

soft soul hard sell
knife wound a catchy name
son found **hanging in the kitchen**
perhaps a **gunshot** to the tiny face
or **car accident** roll over play dead
new name new game or older shame
so on this day when the sun shines red
we the undersigned will agree wholly and
unholy to follow that new booze treaty we
firstly drink this slightly poisonous mostly
white bottle pre-treaty cure all elixir that
gets more expensive when you get older
then take this quill pig pen dip it in blood
india inksnake oil and lawyer lubricant ooze
do not listen to the translator do not read
words that wash off so easily just sign here
put your totem your mark your children here
c'mon just put your

X X X

here
roll up your sleeve and here is your medal sign
quick inject onto paper all that you care for all
these following pillars agreed with the booze treaty:

john le scat (his mark: ✠)

david stole some (his mark: ✶)

see drams for sale (totem: ◯)
no witnesses available

we nailed a treaty to a wall
a new menu

appetizers

mallard fingers – "foie bush," a favourite among indian agents,

they like getting the finger

potato red skins – better than tobacco pouch

salads

birch bark and money greens – apparently, this is edible

chiefs salad – cold, cheap, and costly

main courses

chocolate moose – you follow a moose for days,

when she lifts her tail . . .

welfare red plate special – nothing

mcPemmican – guaranteed berries from this decade

mercury fish – a favourite with three-eyed young 'uns

wannabe wolverine cutlet – garnished red

wilde rice – grown in gaol by certified wagon molesters

desserts

moose cookies – see chocolate moose

ice on the walls cream – wood stove reality

buffalo jello – ask your waiter, Cliff

clown: we must look at the paper

me: the daily shyster

paper scraping

what document leaves

behind

how words can

sink surface to

submarine thoughts

u haul   u gloat   u canoe

why an ex is too dangerous   when poets

dig
too

deep

how about

paper turds

hide scrape   scrape hair   get

bald

palimpsestuous   picto   petro

graph

scribe left behind unknown path

legend treaty remains gathers in balls

layers pousse word café spills

over bush meta four fore for

4444

clown: when do we examine you
me: as long as the grass grows

Red Hiway Poem

They expected me to quit school at 16
So I did
Spectacularly

They told me
Auto mechanic, boy
Nice dirty work
Lotsa cars

Meanwhile I drive like shit
I am pavement danger
My licence comes from the land

& the cops on the red hiway
hate this explanation:

let's see, my driver's licence is from the NWT, my plates from Alberta,

the insurance from god knows where, and this is my buddy's car from

Manitoba.

I long for the days before computer gods.

My licence, gone thru the wash
Crumpled piece paper shit.

> Back of the car: red strobes strobe
> Back of the line: the cop's probes probe.

Gotta make a new treaty on the red hiway.
Gotta make my chief a deal.
Need new hiways on the
RED HIWAY WAY HI
WAY HI
HI WAY
HOOOOO

clown: time for the city
me: that is where I live
the city band

cig poem at the fix

Talk to 70s main street stories

Free for all, free for nobody, bar brawls

Cops too smart, too scared, to go inside

If U made it out you got arrested

So U fight your way to that corner, that desperate corner

People milling main street style

Shark circling   rolling drunks

Getting that role back all in the same night

70s main line town

some way how vibes alive

main event Saturday night

cruise crowds leather   cruise broken glass

fix that thought   fix that cigarette

talk of main

albert street
fix

cig poem

Int. – mcPemmican – always

                    clown: time for a smoke
                                time for
                          another mask
                                time for
                          you to write
                          t r e a t y

Nicotine Whore

In a former life I was a nicotine whore

Wife weaner

Wiener after divorce

I slam poems off the wall

My stepdad *really hates me*

My shrink kicked his kid's ass and left town

The prescription lady will not deliver to this address

Pizza guys, eyes colour frightened, make me come to the car

My social worker goes out tattoo guy

They both hate me too

My welfare check bounced

Life is
good in the Furby street

arson spring of '99

                          clown: look inside
                          the mask that
                          is answer
                          look inside this too

my chicken lies   **over the ocean**

my wife left me for just about anybody

my dog is freaking stupido

my hair farts oil during job interviews

my employment border lines skid row

so bring back   bring back

my chicken for me

so I can sleep

me: they took our chicken, man
clown: uh huh

crow talk

there always been talk of crow
ted hughes   robert kroetsch   so many others
write in crow

salute the big ass voice stalking from the tree

there is a crow movie   the crow tv scene   what is next
son of crow?   crow goes to hollywood?
crow the sequel
the native tribe

crow talk
jars your
head wakes
up the
lazy
things

this year pay attention

the year of the crow

raw caw   cool slaw   not even choctaw

just commercial crows cash in

a crow cartoon used to be

black

when you eat crow
it bites

your throat when you imitate

you get all alone
shotgun wishes
shoot back
thinking crows talk

make someone   tree close
closer to the cacophony   so listen to the poet crows
just do not feed them
crows long for the street

Street smiles

there are street smiles that can get you burned on a drug deal

there are street gardens where kids find a

finger growing

pointing to the clouds   giving the world the finger

there are 25 street smiles you better learn when you

sell your body

there are street faces on every evening petal
that shines black   when the cops keep driving by

that special smile of a chocolate street
melting sunlight

blend incandescent
rain reflects asphalt faces

because u are a
junky fraud

because you really want to just go

home
& play in a garden where the petals do not bite
where the fingers fold in prayer
where the smile heals eyes
burnt by too much evening

by no visible morning

there are smiles melted into the
pavement
by those shiny white body paints
that innovative new urban art genre
marking soul
turf
those Hiroshima   hero shadows
that urge 25 feet into the ground
up rumbles 25 feet
tramping

chocolate gardens for the kids
disappear into mushroom sun

chocolate petals for the young
for old experienced love that still dares

and
and
for that lonely junky fraud
carrying that chocolate smile

on that evening
street

clown: do poets only anger write
me: roses are read
and so
am
I

spread the word

I thought he was going to let me

spread the word   instead

he tries to spread my sister's

legs   so I spread 4 ten shot gun off red

truck neck

off his rapidly retreating down

gravel road   preacher ass   I'm gonna get u snap

button   cowboy ass alberta son of a bastard press a ton of

man

ing   crash test slummy   he never came

never came back   did not rise from the dead

and my sister

kicks his

"wanna go for a coke" routine

into the owl river

walk on water u city oil

slick

spread the word

to the

white

fish tonite

clown: look first

EDGEWALKER

we all walk edges uncertain

on border slippery

between dirt poor

and filthy rich

between Heart   Brake tears

crying in the snow

and sandy beach hot laughter

between bush and city

street bus and the moose track

point out edges that cut off our mind

from the crack baby

cracking smiles at college bank account
we edge walk thin tenuous thread that dangles both
death and birth

edge of eyes of ears of our nose
shows
which edge we want to walk
society edges the other from others

walks all over our person
reality
invisible borders stronger than
barb wire

cement our paths to our edge walking ways
do u rent
or do u own
is the biggest edge
that makes some fall off

economic cliffs
cash lemmings crowd rush hours
and hours and hours
rush whores
run blind to stay on the uptown edges
where
the others
edge their lawns with beer bottle brown
where others
lost that edge
where others close the

bleeding edges of their eyes

by now the media must gather and make headlines that
shout make footlines that slither all of the many words slither words
lost their skin snake treaties lose their spark flash bulb memory
like custer last stand like death crazy horse

crazier world like birth white
buffalo like beothuk remains fighting attention like big bear like
those who sign treaty

yellow head journalism by those witnesses
those interpreter those sir-vey-oars
those sharpened stakes unlike
anything ever seen before words on paper not aural not oral not heard

only herd of settlers
miners: it's all mine loggers: tree T for me
rum alphabet run rabbit fonts until that new breed medicine

man cat bush doctor

that

influence

medium

PULLING FACES

Pull off your face
Underneath lies a Pirandello mask

And under that   Death mask lurks loudly

Colour shifty shapes edges blur   Slippery pictures delight

Pull your face in a little   Red red wagon   That you show to the world
One face for your friends   One for trevor   One for that job application

Now that is one helluva mask   Go paint your face hollow

Certain colours scream bright   Stripes   divide   definite
Region synthetic cool   Paint   the thinnest mask

Could be hooker red   Warrior green trickster blue
Paint the oldest disguise   Belladonna delight
blinding   Fools nobody's god only Your
selves know how many layers   Pile upon skin
brown back Drop eyes light this human Stage
So pull your mind face to the Thoughts of
others Pull faces from history Into today
carny images Pull family faces   into
museum fodder   Art   gallery
features Acrylic dream   masks
for those to follow keep pulling
that face   Down the street
Down down town Down
most roads   And
Down most

coughing

roads
.

me: where is the treaty going
clown: remember what the people go
through

the gant prairie

that day they made us fence through the water
our hunger drove those posts deep   four days till
payday   we make dark lean jokes

gaunt bodies become the gant prairie

what for lunch never spoken word
mustard sandwiches   lukewarm water
offered with a smile
hunger lash   cruel barbs   wire

three days before payday
joke becomes true
sleep thru lunch
hot hamburger dreams
boss places water   end of the line
hot sun bleeds hunger

two days before payday
we catch a crow   better dark chicken
three crow   one gant sandwich

good thing   we brought pepper

salt (treaty)   for the tail   fore man fore skin

crow under tin   fried on a shovel

one day till payday   we find the right moss

tea for coffee break   passed all around

green and strong and free

gant prairie boys boil

tomorrow dreams

then the big day sparkles

arrange ride fateful to town

speak neon cash

share a smoke   gant promise

pay back that loan

long faced boss

loses control

pride

in

roughing

it

then

dark cloud

emergency

we hold two weeks back

don't you know

WHY SO GANT

barb wire

nails him deep post

sets a fire

the job is

over on

this gant

prairie

me: this is a true 70s legend
tell it to all your selves

clown: the 1870s?

sometimes I jump

off roofs tease

the chief

graphic sex

graphic

I also must

make the

people

laugh

                                        me: my next piece is called
                                    that most famous elizabethan
                                            native actor or

BNA ACTOR

[PULL OUT RED SKULL (from captain america) RED
INJUN BOOK, PASS BOOK TO THE AUDIENCE]
                          I have many roles

                          treaty busting is like

                          a full time job, man, so

                       time for some shakey spear

                          [BRANDISH SPEAR]

                          I am most famous

        buckskin role   frontier gig   fall off the damn horse too

                          [FIDDLE WITH SKULL]

                          They call me

                          Omelette!

                          to drink or

                          not to drink

                          that is the question

                       whether tis noble savage to

                      suffer the arrows and arrows

                          of outrageous VLTs

                     or to take one arm bandits

                        into a sea of casinos

                      and end by opposing them?

to drink

nay to party no more

and end the heartache and

the thousand unnatural shocks when you watch that

B movie   over and over

celluloid omelette rejects fries

bush from your brain

[BIG PAUSE]

freeway wagons circle

those hiways were not free

to drink or not to drink

a dime novel story

a type of stereo

typing away your 1860s

persona into that sunset

where wagons burn

john wayne runs out of bullets

where tonto gets a day job

hiawatha goes

bye − a − wa − tha

where the young man who west

goes back where he came from

where christopher columbus sails the ocean Blue

and the santa maria gets drunk and takes chris to Aunt

Arctica instead

think about it, man, indian pen

guins, man, red and white noble penguins, man

drunken fucken penguins, man, the only good penguin is a

dead penguin, man

just think what if columbus had discovered himself instead

so to drink   to drink

there's the rubbie walking down Main

doing that santa maria shuffle

elizabethan red must be tragedy where you talk to skulls

dead invade your living room ghosts

of dead fathers die over and over on those late

nite reruns

so the ghost of Omelette still scrambles after all these years

so let us chase those freaking

winnibagles off a cliff let us bury those drunken skulls

dig   up some new ones   this could be the skull of a

lawyer of the jester   a joker   a clown   a new age trickster

fooling us over and over we see through skull eyes

[PULL APART A SKULL   FIND A POEM]

it is time for the dumb show the ancient legend the real

thing written with big hair eagle

claw

it starts way up there

[HAND OVER EYES, POINT]

one man gets to feet he sees the eagle

he feels the feather grow

he feels the wind rip his thoughts

he totters on the edge of clouds

he flaps his arms he flaps his arms some more

his partner up there his buddy

does not have to flap cuz

for the first time since they invented twist top beer

he is sober

meanwhile flapping away he skywalks he jumps his heart

soars

I AM EAGLE I AM EAGLE I AM EAGLE

(thank u, yuri g.)

THUD!

no, you are not

thank you

very much

[TAKE OFF BONNET AND BOW]

me: about time you act like a clown

Guy on park bench

Slouch park bench alone sitter

Other benches booked sleeper

Another

Definitely the other

Puts the claim on the bench

He is the most alone of all

So alone the mosquitoes do not bite him

Moss points him south So freaking alone, man, panhandlers

look down upon him, man

So alone he gets no food bank

Stagger sidewalks with bruise

Wander universe erratic, invisible blazed trails

Stay downtown man

The bush will arrest you

Stay sleeping bench man

U do not want to wake this reality

Do not wake up so alone   man

INT. / EXT. – a heart

t-bird chapel

t-bird chapel

lord thundering jesus bird

open for business

drums for sale   drums for sale

come one come all

wire on a   bird dress

t-bird flies away   all colour   precious gone

chapels need cash

cash needs that t-bird

I need a job

virtual indian

stir and shake
b movie western

add some tonto
a bit of apache   some ojicree   some navajo   some aztec

a little new age shuffle
the noble
sauvage

shake a captive
narrative slow into the mix

the last of the wood
stove memories

the electric indian rides tall
john ford john doe run johnny run

tee pee motel
beckons

unemployed cigar store stiffs mill downtown

fat emma melts away

to be virtual

to be electric organic

when you live inner

city feathers plastic

motorcycle mascot

grain gasoline

no more virtue

when

artificial

never chopped wood

virtually only

when buffalo were nuclear free
before gunpowder buffalo
had this attitude
just go in a straight line
life was good
before screen savers buffalo
rumble four step dance cliff
after a-bomb
buffalo
got small

first job poem

other than chopping

hauling

wood horse dragging

water heaviness pail

bucket slave

& beer bottle picking

the first pay job

one that paid regular basis

one that bought smokes   new friends trouble

my first job was loading racks

pulp wood bonanza

75 cents a rack

guys quitting   enough for a 6 pak

midnite sometimes   the trucks came in

somehow in the snow

never thought I would like this

memory cig poem

Panama jack

riot on portage ave

cuz Panama jack is back in town

international style

empty stomach stretches marks across the americas

jump both sides of that Panama Canal

who gets the gold?

who came first?

the chicken?

or, no chicken tonite

Panama jack soaks his feet in 45-gallon drum

he's sort of a Huck Finn on drugs

his eyes feel those bootleg body parts burning

constant walking to survive

Panama cases the tourists

all too fat for sidewalk bungalow

money tied to a stick

dance, boy, dance!

dance that Panama jack dance that the people love

so well

Make those feet go up the wall and come down,

Boy.

now Panama soaks his feet in coke cans, one for each toe, cool

and refreshing feet

must step out the pattern

walk sideways on that broken glass

slide blood from one foot to the other so nobody sees

that red red line across the americas

so dance, Panama, dance

before it's too late

              clown: why did the crow cross the road

Jam Cig Poem

I want to jam this poem up that cop's ass

back seat puncher

who wants u to confess

wants u to b & e

meaning broke and evil

we had jam

way too much jam

jam christianity down northern outhouse black hole

cop spits out

my blood shot eyes

(basically partied in the 70s)

my bloodfreakingshot eyes

gave his body chills down and up

after we pissed blood in the alley

me and mike

true blood brothers

sat in this twenty-four joint nursing that bit of coffee

till that waitress jams us some smokes

in exchange for street story

she was kool she was real

we were too sore to laugh

running rain sticky one way ticket jam

train station grit

life segment in the ditch

jam those people memories foggy sidewalk

jam those cop eyes with this

jammin' cig poem

White Settlers

maybe in the 60s

the 1860s

There exists

In the language of the english

Two words all powerful

Fury terrible terrible

Nuclear thinking

Those two words

That catalyst sound pair

Makes red blood boil and hiss

WHITE SETTLERS

See the reaction

Go down any street

Pick any native

She could be a lawyer

He could be a doctor

They could be indian chiefs (chives? cheeves?)

Mention those settlers careful

Careful and slow

Feel the reaction

Building

Smouldering

Exploding

Across that john ford land scape

MASSACRE
ATTACK AT DAWN
MAIN STREET is burning

BURN BABY BURN
HATCHET CITY, MAN

TOMAHAWK TUNES, MAN OH MAN
KILL KILL KILL
MURDER MUTILATE MAYHEM!
SCALP THEIR STUBBLE ASSES
SCALP THEIR GRANDMAS
SCALP THEIR BARBERS
SCALP DISNEY, MAN
AND SKIN Bambi
And HOPPED UP CASSIDY

DISFIGURE THOSE STUBBLE DREAMS

Fuk u john wane
Clint westwood

Bonanza bonus at the KO KORRAL
FUK U ALONE RANGER

Circle your wagon wheels u
Bible ass preacher residential school dictator
those relentless plows tearing our mother

SO
LET'S PLAY SMALL POX BLANKET BINGO

Under the B: BYE BYE NATIVE GUY U GOT THE POX

Under the I: I got scars under my eyes

Under the N: NATIVE VERSUS SETTLER, THE SEQUEL

Under the G: gone with the wind A   RHEA

Under the O: Oh, boy, oh, oh, oh no, I am freaking dead, man
And finally

BINGO!!!!!!!!
Fuck your colonial euro-attitude dudes
Your post colonial angst

Fuck mohawk gas
Atlanta braves
Cleveland indians
Washington redskins
THE KANSAS CITY CHIEFS

And especially
One little
Two little
Three little
Indians
All in a big pile on top of that

Cigar store stoic stupidity

Fuck the noble and not so noble
Savage lost in the B movie

Lost in the glare fenimore
cooper fantasy drunk in the tee

pee motel

The cree pee
hotel

settler wall paper   antler velvet rubs

settles whitesunset

unsettled red

me: Jesus! this will get us Grant
(and more than one
army)

clown: you don't write
treatypoems for the money
you make waves

native tempest

"they will lay out ten to see a dead Indian" shakey spear

nabilac sits at fire   always contrary

birch heat brother   burns

company   smoke squirms

waits for magicians to arrive

they make land disappear

he shouts: *"the red plague rid you*

for learning me your language"

treaty language

easy translate

you will lose

"you taught me language   I know how to curse"

words only count

1 little 2 little 3 little 4 little   indian boys

and then there were none

(ask agatha)

extinct tribes lost land gauge

lost children   trail of beers

nabilac burns   paper treaty trails

    the smoke is white   the crackle electric

                        "all the infections that the sun sucks up"

no wonder the sun so volatile

    uncommon cold words

flu out the window   *"wicked due"*

spots face   spots son spotted

    thou shall be pinched

In event of emergency: SEND IN THE DOGS

(clowns make trouble)

              "thy dog and thy bush"

that shakey spear knew his tempests

                  EXT. – treaty site – 100 dog years ago

    a pipe goes hand to mouth   the truth must be spoken

    words scrape paper instead   word hustlers gather   the

                                     squirrels trap

                                     back this year

more treaty lines
1790 → *treaty 2, district of Hesse (step into wolf)*
province of quebec
"We do hereby certify that the following goods were delivered to the
several Nations"

list

to one side   jousting   a stripe of colour

35 pieces of Strouds
(coarse from england)

1 dozen black silk handkerchiefs
(the first head bands in the hood
did the chiefs take them in hand)

20 dz. plain hats
(plains indian hats)

40 nests of tin kettles
(they sign the treaty
they want to raise tin
birds)

60 guns
20 rifles
400 lbs. powder
1,600 lbs. ball and shot
2,000 flints
(rabbit hell)

30 dz. looking glasses
(piece of hard hard water everyone must see)

Aboriginal refraction
Life reflection
Indigenous carol
Cast through the holes
Expressionistic glass

clown: I still remember my first looking glass
me: I still shave with a piece of tin foil

Lee Eegle Eze

were-ass
hereto and
forthwith
know all men by these presents
undersigned
said party
said indian
cede transfer relinquish surrender
solemnly
yield up
certain
chains across west links north lynx
south due
east more
or less
chains word tract lying to the place
of be
ginning
a line
drawn for the band lots said limit
strip of
land of
broken
lots whence occupy as a reserve thence
legal
eagle
flies

from lofty perch from the defined
territory
bound
aerie
proviso authorised designated virtue
power of
attorney
forty
arpents frontage zero arpent depth
as straight
as any
eegle flies

✈✈✈✈✈✈✈✈✈✈✈✈✈✈✈✈✈✈✈

clown: everything its own language
even rig pigs   the words
those lost languages   hide the meaning

business talk
level playing field

land natural invent
sound
escape

language comes
from the
land

so many words for
snow

no words describe
agony of kids
torn a way

of
your language

sudden
illegal

equals ill eagle

of hair cuts

of

standing in the
closet

THIS GUN IS THIS TALL

What fur said those trappers do we have to pile these so high   when we paddle paddle paddle blood   to get here when we follow those animals   when we apprentice for ten thousand years   so you can get your beaver hat   and *how* come these guns are so tall the fur so short *how* come all of the northern stores so much fur you not fur us why do you think this is your territory henry? why don't you have any place left to set traps will your fashion always feed my kids the sound of this gun drowns the sound of the land the smell of the trader gives beaver night mare the touch of steel chills the soul freezes the north the taste of your justice sours my snares does the animal spirit make the london man about town sexy or does the hat substitute for the high number of victorian hookers who fish for life just like we have learned how high you can pile this pissed off fur traitor about what high what fur

we meta in the corral

we fall off white roofs together   we met in the corral

we fell off white roofs together

meat corrals
(overheard in native singles meat
packing circles)

we corral meat

the clown began to paint

we met duster tradition

everyone west of that spot on transcanada trans like
transculture hitch hyke diesel assed hiway must face
that face

heavy (beer belly)
duty face
dirty whisker
probably whiskey

old time good old back up against the   moment
gotta put up the DUKE (while falling onto horse)

sort of like that native don cherrie:

DAWN SASKATOON

kick in the head
hard on the gpa
worse the next morning
it hurts to win too

fight

scrap   like torn clothing

take the gloves off   keep those ball caps close

two fighters circle

nobody wants to

lose

meet saturday night   corral roots:

THE FACE OFF!

hockey as standard

how the fuck did that ever happen   ?↑↓?

toothless role models breed hardy

now known forever as

high moon

just knew that a duel was coming

never create art with another

clown enters corral armed with

ten thousand oral stories

falling off old tongues

all bush dialect   camp fire literary

I dragged a dictionary
through the mud
street thesaurus

walk: n. =
1. no! don't walk like that,
else, somebody mugs you,
don't walk like a victim

2. never! walk into a bar like you own it

unless you do.

                                        word hurling
                                        in your face

                              but some words feather
                              across the banks of the river:
                                        Running Bare

                                        stripped down
                                        buck naked

    . . . .*and on the udderrrrr side of   duh riveRrrr*. . . . .

                              (YEAH YEAH, been there, I know)
MEANWHILE,
BACK AT THE
CORRAL

            painted circle dominates domestic manure
    painted horse, just like tonto's horse, van gogh sorrel, picasso
                    bronc, morriseau horse eyes,
                        odjig mare

                        paintPOEM

                eye duel begins nose to nose
                    the fight must go on

            barrage word learned meets the clown

                            and
                            then

            the risky birth of muskeg metaphor
        moss verbiage   north side of the canon / cannon
                south of the profit margin

                rabbit critics got nothing to lose

peter rabbit for lunch

wolverine essays rend wordsworth

shoveller ducks migrate shakespeare

hamlet flies in the shape of a

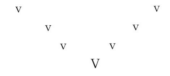

```
  v                          v
      v                  v
          v      v
              V
```

virginia is allowed to howl wolf
a different howl
not ginsberg
not lear

a bush of my own
waiting for pogey check
my camp fire burns at both ends
I wandered only as red cloud
a gentle dynamite was pricking on the prairie
it was the west of the Times
it was the cursed in the Times
from the unrude the smoketh of a poets (snow) blind

we met (a) corral   circle in square

word cannibal

look at small pox petro glyphs

little crosses   the americas

graffiti dreams
aerosol glyph

buffalo were vegetarian
paint was a plant

radiation grass
pigment

from all this   those word cannibals, those freaking word
cannibals, they..............

stole my words

man, if you eat other people's words you are capable of
anything
                but some sneaky
                slithering words
            lie hidden in the bush
        some walk down fear strutting streets

    words youth survival: don't walk this way in the pool hall

        don't hitchhike both ways on the highway

need some language insurance
                dialect alarm system
                        somewhere in the land

that clown hides dirt
dig furious badger pissed off gopher

"there used to be a lot of adolescent gopher murderers in this
country"
said at breakfast the next morning
the clown had a new haircut attitude
sunshine loves sunshine

who is the clown
who is the clown
who is the clown

land gurgles red panorama

picto-chickens   cling on   rocks   pecking orders
from that boss man/look at   I'm   cool/kinda   clown

we moved the treaty site
we felt the natural

(the right instruments must be chosen
the right words spoken before I will follow)

clown and me   back to back

trust those circles
I knew now it was

that time

to write that

city treaty

      days of preparation/ gathering <powwow>
latched right onto the necessary tools

           rub the land onto every treaty
        do not poison all we got do not poison

name local proud names

CUT TO:

(Subsection b, wherein, etc. etc. see city treaty)

new INDIAN GUIDE

go clean your own fish you lazy fucks

tourists lost in fish fly tornado
knee deep beer bottles go back to town

trout rainbow poems instead
try to catch those little black hair snakes
some peoples call them thread snakes
they were cool swampy
always let them go

make red devil hook jewellery
fishermans not
plugs bobbers leaders perch waits

DISSOLVE TO: INTERLEWD

we cut the cards to see who goes first
there were no queens kings knaves
we were all jokers

I drew the seven of clowns
The clown drew the seven
we tie again
so
shuffle shuffle shuffle shuffle shuffle
a head held high shuffle
heart lake cards with corners all bent couple of cards missing
a hybrid of old and new
"marked" by some loser with felt pen
the joker always the favourite

we draw together
a new card every wonderful time
card tricks with coal oil lamp

we read a card
hold it up high

the little ones come first
the little ones come first

put that in the treaty and smoke it
the little ones come first

treaty adhesions

(or, bush glue)

    no more drunk words

    you cannot lie in a treaty

    many languages, customs, environments, have to be included

    everyone has some voice

if it doesn't fit into your back
pocket don't trust it

stick on changes/add/subtract/all sides
paste layer upon
       layer of
thought

bury the pseudo shaman in piles of pain

argue/bitch/question/probe/tear apart/challenge/discuss until
everyone is sick of it, then do it again for you have
to *remember what the people went through*

FLASHBACK

circle of a people with their   hearts in the fire their spirit
in the

                    smoke their
       minds in the crackle their guts hanging out
           with knowledge for

      flash back to those treaties smouldering
           collecting our dust

flash forward too and loop all the different time zones
accordian

flash present to disguise like as tree
as a comic book flashsuit in a
ring
cool

thru the flashing backs over and under and around

the clown and I sit
back to back
in the suns
how to write a
treaty who cares
recall the names
of your ancestors
remember the
names that you
got called

some beer labels I once knew

reality tv demands   reality advertising
blurred reality
new beer labels:

divorce home maid barley sand which goes down glossy,

nag mag ads

fas beer breeds copy righters who can write anything

runaway ale for those young who ail all nite long and

cannot fight back

flat broke this fine pilsner is already flat but you drink it
anyways cuz your heart is broken and nobody
will drink from the same bottle as you

loser sold everywhere in quart king cans

and at last bobbing its head

above the brown waves the ultimate reality beer bursts onto the
scene in
every beach party every camp site

and all the house parties the fancy cock
tail circuit
this beer has poetic license

have yourself a

smelly drunk for that long long road long
gone home

I pick my guitar tunes the clown picks finger nails
we were on a break we had knowledge
that native landscapes contain
asphalt
back onto our
feet again

treaty map

to cover all of the territory the treaty must be as large as the
land itself like a borges map   we cover the land find the
paper stretcher   reach all the borders   use the word
manglers   make sound that contours land   the witness has
chip munk approval   the requisite coyote copy right   every
shrub tree and plant has geographical importance   which was
always on our map   allow seasonal migration   human to city
and back   while rivers wash inside   the prairie undulates the
canadian shield up one side of the rockies and down the
mackenzie   so you can finally figure out that this land   is
owned by your children   never by you   so me and this
clown   drag
                this treaty map   overland   overwater   overair

                        and we sit
                        me and this clown
                        and now have
                        just recently begun
                        to right

                        the city treaty

                        Joe TB
                picks himself off the ground
                        the rust gone from
                        word spurs
                        the treaty got
                        busted

                while off to the side

                like rodeo clown acrobat

treaty parts   pieces blow empty   thoughts

the prairie sunset
still pretty in the
city the gopher
silhouette rains

a sound shakes
ear to the ground
like buffalo watch dazzle
all wonder   hope
something must be followed too   some thing feels good
me: what is this thing and the clown's eyes begin to water
tells me to listen
boom boom
(not the hockey player)
here come the leaders the mavericks who cannot shut up

word drummers

so many drum sticks flash

momaday takes us to rainy mountains   joy of horses joe
(king and hiway)   break open the way   erdrich
narrative willow twists annaharte frankensquaw opens eye
while mcnickle gets surrounded maracle vancouver tears the
heart   armstrong slashes canlit within the same silko
ceremony   jordan wheels tv   while drew some
curve lake laughs   alexis gives us famous fistfight
vizenor theory sizzles   the bad dog trudell   crunch
bernice half bones   as duncan mixes it
all together in his traditionalist stew

many stubborn writers
poet   playwright   screenwriter

short story   long novel   tall tales camp fire palimpsest legends
ancient rumours novellas   petroglyph hypertext syllabics
                     prose poem
longpoem   skit character sketch   first person last in line
                   point of view
               the landscape now has city

     walk in the bush narrative: up   then down   around a tree
sink in the muskeg   heave frost splinters   dodge a bear
               so there are no linear no
               straight lines in the bush
               the city only thinks so
          follow the word drummers to the city treaty

   those word drummers pound away and hurtle
words into that english landscape like brown beer
bottles tossed from the back seat on a country
road shattering the air   turtle words crawl slowly from
the broken glass

                                        me and the
                                   clown caught some
                                   well deserved sleep

   fade out   *fade out*   fade out